Author:
Jacqueline Morley studied English literature at Oxford University. She has taught English and history and now works as a freelance writer. She has written historical fiction and nonfiction for children.

Artist:
David Antram was born in Brighton, England, in 1958. He studied at Eastbourne College of Art and then worked in advertising for 15 years before becoming a full-time artist. He has illustrated many children's nonfiction books.

Series creator:
David Salariya was born in Dundee, Scotland. He has illustrated a wide range of books and has created and designed many new series for publishers in the UK and overseas. David established The Salariya Book Company in 1989. He lives in Brighton with his wife, illustrator Shirley Willis, and their son, Jonathan.

Editor: **Tanya Kant**

Editorial Assistant: **Mark Williams**

© The Salariya Book Company Ltd MMX

Published in Great Britain in 2010 by
The Salariya Book Company Ltd
25 Marlborough Place, Brighton BN1 1UB

ISBN-13: 978-0-531-20471-9 (lib. bdg.) 978-0-531-22826-5 (pbk.)
ISBN-10: 0-531-20471-5 (lib. bdg.) 0-531-22826-6 (pbk.)

All rights reserved.
Published in 2010 in the United States
by Franklin Watts
An imprint of Scholastic Inc.
557 Broadway, New York, NY 10012
Published simultaneously in Canada.

A CIP catalog record for this book is available from the Library of Congress.

Printed and bound in Shanghai, China.
Printed on paper from sustainable sources.
Reprinted in MMXVI.
3 4 5 6 7 8 9 10 R 18 17 16

SCHOLASTIC, FRANKLIN WATTS, and associated logos are trademarks and/or registered trademarks of Scholastic Inc.

PAPER FROM
SUSTAINABLE
FORESTS

You Wouldn't Want to Be a Shakespearean Actor!

Some Roles You Might Not Want to Play

Written by
Jacqueline Morley

Illustrated by
David Antram

Created and designed by
David Salariya

Franklin Watts®
An Imprint of Scholastic Inc.
NEW YORK • TORONTO • LONDON • AUCKLAND • SYDNEY
MEXICO CITY • NEW DELHI • HONG KONG
DANBURY, CONNECTICUT

Contents

Introduction 5

Burbage's First Theater 6

Joining the Company 8

Your Big Chance 10

A Working Day 12

Stretching Your Memory 14

The Plague 16

On the Road 18

Christmas Crisis 20

The Globe 22

Backstage at the Globe 24

Fire! 26

A Roof Over Your Head 28

Glossary 30

Index 32

Introduction

It's 1594 and you're a young boy growing up in Shoreditch, a neighborhood on the outskirts of London. Until about 20 years ago, it was a quiet spot. Then actors from the city arrived and put up a "playhouse" here—a building just for putting on plays! Before this, actors—who are called players—had always traveled the country, setting up makeshift stages wherever they could find an audience.

Puritans, like your parents, don't approve of acting. They say that players don't do real work—they just play. They also say that plays are just longer versions of the foolish shows that wandering entertainers have been putting on since medieval times. But you think your parents are wrong to say that plays are displeasing to God; they've never been to one! Well, you have (unknown to them, of course), and you think plays are the best thing ever. You'd love to act in one.

▲ *Medieval entertainers*

◀ *16th-century players*

Burbage's First Theater

In 1576, James Burbage, the manager of a company of players, opened a playhouse in Shoreditch and named it "The Theatre."

It's been a huge success. The London area has several "theaters" now (the term has caught on), but the most exciting plays are at Burbage's. His company is now called "The Lord Chamberlain's Men," and his son Richard is a great actor. One of the other players is a brilliant writer as well. His name is William Shakespeare. One day, he'll be known as the world's most famous playwright.

THE COURTYARDS of London's inns were once used for plays, but people complained about the rowdy audiences. So London authorities banned playing in inns.

BEAR-BAITING arenas had given Burbage an idea—build a large, round theater, like a bear-baiting ring, with an open central yard to hold audiences.

Grrrr!

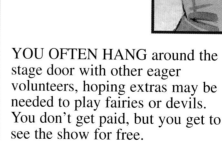

Pick me!

No, pick me!

Hail!

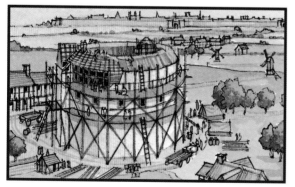

BURBAGE rented land in Shoreditch, just beyond London's city boundaries, where the ban on plays doesn't apply. He built a playhouse that could hold much bigger audiences than an inn yard.

YOU OFTEN HANG around the stage door with other eager volunteers, hoping extras may be needed to play fairies or devils. You don't get paid, but you get to see the show for free.

A BOY PLAYER has fallen sick, so a volunteer is needed—and Burbage picks you! It's only a small part in Shakespeare's play *A Midsummer Night's Dream*, but it's a dream come true for you.

7

Joining the Company

You soon realize that theater life is tough. As the owner of the theater, old James Burbage gets over half the takings. Leading company members share the rest, and minor players make do with meager wages. You're an apprentice, so you get nothing—though if times are good, Richard Burbage might slip you a little money. He's training you to move and speak like a woman, so that you can play female roles. Women aren't allowed to act—it's considered improper. Young boys play the female roles instead. When you're ready, you'll get to go on stage. Burbage will also hire you out to other companies that need young actors.

Now is the winter of our discontent...

APPRENTICES have to earn their keep by doing chores. You fetch and carry things for the players and help clean up after performances.

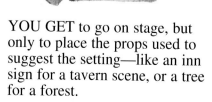

YOU GET to go on stage, but only to place the props used to suggest the setting—like an inn sign for a tavern scene, or a tree for a forest.

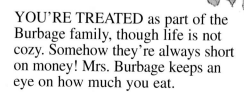

YOU'RE TREATED as part of the Burbage family, though life is not cozy. Somehow they're always short on money! Mrs. Burbage keeps an eye on how much you eat.

Stand up straight! Ladies never slouch!

YOU LEARN to stay out of old James Burbage's way. He's often in a bad mood, especially if the takings are poor or if he has debts to pay.

THERE WAS a big fight when Burbage's business partner accused him of stealing the company's takings. The money was kept in a box with two locks. Each partner had a key to only one lock, so neither man could open the box alone. Yet money was missing!

Dirty swindler! You've copied my key!

Your Big Chance

You've been doing small parts for a while now, and Richard Burbage thinks you're ready for a major role. Shakespeare has just come up with a new play—*Love's Labour's Lost*.

It's sure to be a hit. You are playing the Princess of France. It's not the lead role, but you still have to be good! The worst part is the costume fitting—hours spent standing with tiremen (assistants who help you dress) yanking you into a metal-stiffened corset and a horrible farthingale (a metal frame that fills out your skirt).

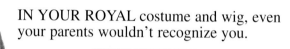

IN YOUR ROYAL costume and wig, even your parents wouldn't recognize you.

RATS ARE the tiremen's worst enemy. They've gnawed the hem of the cloak that you'll be wearing. You're sent out to buy some copper lace to patch it up.

FOR GOING OUTSIDE the theater in costume, you get a whopping fine. Costumes are often hand-me-downs from real nobles and are very valuable—so don't damage yours!

Handy Hint

To avoid making a sensational unplanned appearance, practice walking in your skirt and heels.

Corset

Farthingale

A Working Day

After morning rehearsals, the leading players gather to hear Shakespeare read from his latest play—*Romeo and Juliet*. He reads out some lines and they sound good, so the company decides to buy the play. You can't believe your luck when Shakespeare suggests that you play Juliet. The role could launch your career.

But your big break makes life difficult. Boys who've been acting longer than you are jealous, and learning such a big part is an awful lot of work. You've got some long days ahead of you.

This is not very ladylike!

YOU WAKE UP feeling chilly—the Burbages' attic is far from warm. Last night you were too tired to study your part for today's rehearsal. Better skip breakfast and learn it now.

YOU LOSE TRACK of time trying to learn your lines, and old Burbage catches you coming in late. Now you'll get no pocket money—he'll say it went to pay the fine for lateness.

DURING rehearsal you mess up two speeches. It doesn't help that it's been raining. The stage is open to the sky, and now the floor is slippery. You keep sliding all over the place.

But soft, what light through yonder window breaks? It is the east, and Juliet is the sun!

Handy Hint

There's no such thing as a free lunch. If James Burbage treats the players to a meal, he pays himself back from their share of the takings.

I'll have two large and one extra small.

You're on in five minutes!

REHEARSALS last all morning. Then Richard Burbage sends you to the hot-pie stall to buy him some meat pies for lunch. Usually he gives you enough money so you can have one, too.

ROMEO AND JULIET starts at 2 P.M., but the actor playing Romeo's mother has broken out in a rash! You have to do his part as well as yours. Luckily you only need to learn two lines and draw wrinkles on your face.

TONIGHT the players are giving a private performance. Sometimes you perform for Queen Elizabeth, but tonight you'll play for law students. They're very rowdy—and you long for bed!

13

Stretching Your Memory

You're a star player now, the company's first choice for female leads. But there's a downside to success. You're up till midnight, studying lines until you feel your head will split.

The trouble is, to keep the audiences coming, the company performs a different play each day. There are some 40 plays to choose from, and you must act in all of them. You have to remember every part you've ever learned! About 15 plays a year will be new; the rest are revivals of old plays. In some plays, you perform more than one role, so altogether you need to keep at least 50 parts in your head. Minor actors, who each play more than one part, may need to memorize 100 roles.

COMPANIES pay writers to churn out plays. Most do a sloppy job for little money. Your company is lucky to have Shakespeare writing for it.

EACH PLAY'S text (known as its "book") must be checked by the Office of the Master of the Revels. They make sure there's nothing in it that might offend the queen.

You'll love this one.

IF A PLAY is a hit, its text becomes valuable. It's locked away so rival companies can't use it. Watch out for men in the audience taking notes—they may be making a pirated version.

O Romeo, Romeo…
I can barely keep my
eyes open…

Handy Hint

Tragic roles are easier to learn. Tragedies are written mostly in verse, and the rhythm helps you memorize the lines.

THE BOOKKEEPER is crucial during a performance. He stands backstage and ensures that everything runs smoothly. In his book, he notes each player's moves, as well as the props and sound effects required. If your mind goes blank, he's there to prompt you.

Two bangs and then exit stage left.

The Plague

Each summer, Londoners dread the return of a deadly illness known as the plague. Victims get a sudden fever, and many die just days later. No one knows what causes the plague, but every few years it arrives with the summer heat and seems to get passed on rapidly in crowds. Theaters draw the largest crowds, so they are shut down during bad outbreaks.

This year, you've seen red crosses painted on doors, warning people that these homes are plague-stricken. Death carts rumble through the streets every night, picking up bodies that have been left on doorsteps. It won't be long before play-going is banned.

This is not good for business.

You're a good boy, sonny.

NO ONE is allowed to leave the house of a plague victim. You bring food to trapped relatives.

PEOPLE say bad air causes the plague. Bonfires are lit in the hope that they will purify the air. No one knows that the disease is actually caught from fleas carried by black rats.

Handy Hint

For protection against plague fumes, hold a pomander (a spice-scented ball) to your nose when you go out.

SO MANY PEOPLE have died that it's impossible to give them all funerals. Bodies are piled into pits and sprinkled with lime (a powder that comes from limestone) to hide the smell.

YOUR COMPANY'S wagons join the long lines of Londoners trying to escape the plague. But you're not just fleeing disease—you're seeking work, too.

On the Road

When the plague forces theaters to close, players have to travel—just as they did in the old days. That's not good news for anyone. Audiences in towns and villages will be small, especially if people fear you're bringing the plague with you. Managers need to keep costs down, and many players are fired. Your job is safe because the company needs actors who can play women. But living on reduced pay—and sleeping underneath the wagon—makes you wonder whether this life is worth the trouble.

PUBLICITY is essential. You need to let everyone in town know you've arrived. The whole company parades through the streets, making as much noise as possible.

PLAYERS CAN'T perform without permission from the local mayor. The first town you visit is so afraid of the plague that the mayor pays you to go away.

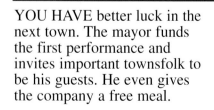

YOU HAVE better luck in the next town. The mayor funds the first performance and invites important townsfolk to be his guests. He even gives the company a free meal.

DURING the mayor's meal, some of the more rowdy players get into a brawl. They end up spending a day in the stocks.

Christmas Crisis

It's 1598 and you've had a terrible year. Old James Burbage passed away in 1597, and the company has been thrown out of The Theatre. The owner of the land it's built on is claiming that The Theatre is his. He says the Burbages were such bad tenants that they've lost their right to it. The players are furious, so they've arranged to have The Theatre dismantled secretly over Christmas. They're going to take its valuable timbers (wooden beams) and build a new playhouse elsewhere! But as the players start dismantling, officials arrive with a writ (written command) ordering the players to stop. A big fight breaks out!

THE COMPANY was thrown out of The Theatre over a year ago. So the players have been using a run-down theater called the Curtain. You made a big impression there in Shakespeare's *Much Ado About Nothing*.

THE FIGHT has not helped Richard Burbage's temper. Like father, like son!

THE TIMBER RAID gives the company what it needs— essential building materials. It has them carted to another site to build a new theater.

21

The Globe

The company has built a new theater in Bankside—an area of London on the south bank of the River Thames. It's called the Globe. Even using the old timbers, the theater cost a lot to build. The leading players put up the money for it, so the Globe is owned by them, not by a manager. Shakespeare is one of the investors, which means you're acting in his theater now. You love life on Bankside. Londoners come here for the taverns, the bear-baiting, and the theaters. Being south of the river means Bankside is outside city control, so anything goes!

THE GLOBE is similar in plan to The Theatre, but grander. People pay a single penny to stand near the stage, two to sit in the galleries, and three for good seats with cushions.

PEOPLE who stand in the yard are called the groundlings. They don't mind standing, but if they dislike the play they'll throw things at you. Let's hope it's only apple cores and nutshells.

"GATHERERS" collect the entrance money (there are no tickets). Some scratch their ears a lot. Are they stealing money by slipping coins down their necks?

Gable

Thatched roof

Gallery

Stage

Staircase

Yard (standing area)

Backstage at the Globe

The years are passing, and for an actor like you—a boy who plays women—time is your enemy. You're too old to play Juliet any longer. Now you play her mother. Backstage in the tiring house—the place where players get into their attire (costumes)—your mirror tells you that you're losing that fragile look. Soon you'll be 18 and too masculine for female roles.

All around you people are rushing about looking for props, adjusting costumes, and calling for the trumpeter to signal the start of the performance. You're no longer the center of attention.

THE GLOBE'S stairway leads to the stage gallery and storerooms. Here there is a pulley that lowers actors playing gods onto the stage from the "heavens."

BAD WEATHER sometimes causes performances to be canceled. Londoners look to see whether the flag is flying above the theater (right). If it is, there'll be a show.

The flag signals that the weather is good enough for a performance.

Handy Hint

Avoid mistakes by checking the "plot" before you go on. It's an outline of the day's play.

I'm going to need more makeup.

Fire!

It's 1613—two decades since you first joined the players. Let's face it, your career has not been a success. The company has made it clear that you're not cut out to be a male lead. Today you have a walk-on part as an attendant to Cardinal Wolsey in Shakespeare's *Henry VIII*. In this scene, the king and his followers have just arrived at Wolsey's feast, disguised as shepherds. The stagehands fire a real cannon, placed in the gable at the top of the theater, to salute the king's approach. While everyone else is looking at the stage, you are so bored that you're staring into space. So you are the first one to notice that the roof is in flames!

Gable

Bang!

I don't remember that line...

I want my money back!

THE THEATER is full. More than 2,000 people head for the doors. There are only two exits, but somehow everyone manages to get out unharmed.

THE ONLY INJURY is to a man whose breeches catch fire. Luckily he has just bought himself a drink, so he puts it to good use.

WHEN THE CANNON was fired, some sparks or smoldering wadding must have landed on the roof and set the thatch on fire. Once the fire gets going, nothing can stop it.

Fire!

Handy Hint

To prevent fire, rebuild the Globe with a tiled roof instead of a thatched one.

THERE'S PLENTY of water on hand in the River Thames, but the only way to carry it to the fire is to pass buckets. (Professional firefighting with pumps is a thing of the future.)

IN TWO HOURS the Globe is burned to the ground. The company decides to rebuild it at once. It reopens in 1614.

27

A Roof Over Your Head

The company's fortunes are improving. Queen Elizabeth died in 1603, and the new king loves plays even more than she did. King James has renamed the company "The King's Men," and it has been allowed to open a theater in the city. It's called Blackfriars—the first indoor theater in London. The company plays there in the winter and at the Globe during the summer.

For you, the future's not so rosy. You get only the old-man roles. You weren't bad as Polonius in *Hamlet*. If you had known things would turn out this way, would you have wanted to be a Shakespearean actor?

BLACKFRIARS is built in an old monastery. There are seats for the whole audience and a roof overhead. It makes the Globe seem old-fashioned. This type of setting is the theater of the future.

Handy Hint

No need to shout your lines at Blackfriars. In a smaller space, you need a subtler acting style.

This above all: To thine own self be true.

Fie, Polonius, that's acting most foul!

BLACKFRIARS draws a rich audience. The gentlemen who sit in the best seats at the side of the stage show off by making irritating comments.

INDOOR theaters need candles. The play stops while they are trimmed, to keep them from going out. (This is how the custom of intermissions began.)

Glossary

Apprentice An unpaid trainee who serves his master for a set number of years in return for learning a skill.

Apprenticeship The position that an apprentice takes.

Attire Clothing, especially a costume.

Bear-baiting A cruel sport that pitted dogs against a chained bear. Bear-baiting was banned in England in 1835.

Bookkeeper In Elizabethan theater, a person who tracks everything that's needed to perform a play.

Breeches A type of men's pants, popular in the 16th century, that reach from the waist to just below the knee.

Company A group of entertainers that perform together.

Cutpurse A thief who cut the straps of the money purses that people in 16th-century England hung from their belts.

Doublet A man's short, tight-fitting jacket, popular in the 16th century.

Farthingale A framework of reed or metal hoops that filled out a woman's skirt.

Gable The triangular part of a wall between the slopes of the roof.

Lord Chamberlain's Men, The The company of players formed in 1594 and later known as the King's Men. Members included William Shakespeare and Richard Burbage.

Master of the Revels The official in charge of organizing royal entertainments and licensing plays.

Monastery A place where Catholic monks live and work. England's monasteries were put to other uses after Henry VIII abolished them in the 1530s.

Player The 16th-century term for an actor.

Playhouse A 16th-century term for a theater.

Pomander A mixture of sweet-smelling spices formed into a ball, often kept in a metal holder hung around the neck.

Props Objects used in a play, such as weapons or furniture.

Puritans Members of a strict Christian group that opposed England's official church in the 16th and 17th centuries.

Rogue A dishonest or troublesome person.

Stage door The door at the rear of a theater that is used by the actors.

Stage gallery A balcony area above the stage that was used by the actors during performances, or by musicians playing music as part of the show.

Stocks A wooden frame with holes in it, used to hold people by their ankles. Stocks were set up in public so prisoners could be humiliated by other townspeople.

Takings The money received from the audience for a play.

Thatch A straw-like material traditionally used to cover roofs.

Tiremen Assistants who helped actors put on their costumes.

Tiring house An area behind the stage where actors got dressed and where costumes and props were stored.

Tragedies Plays that deal with serious subjects and have an unhappy ending.

Trim (of candles) To remove melted wax and cut the wick of a candle so that it will not make too much smoke.

Wadding A piece of cloth that was rammed into a cannon to hold the gunpowder and cannonball in place.

Walk-on part A role that does not involve speaking.

Writ A written order, issued by a court.

Index

A
apprentice 8
apprenticeships 7
audiences 6, 18, 28, 29

B
backstage 15, 24
Bankside 22, 23
bear-baiting 6, 22
Blackfriars theater 28, 29
bonfires 16
bookkeeper 15
Burbage, James ("old Burbage")
  6, 7, 8, 9, 12, 13, 20
Burbage, Mrs. 8
Burbage, Richard 6, 8, 10, 13, 20

C
costume 10, 24
Curtain theater 20
cutpurses 23

F
fine 10, 12
fire 26, 27
firefighting 27

G
gatherers 22
Globe theater 22, 24, 27, 28
groundlings 22

H
Hamlet 28
Henry VIII 26

I
intermissions 29

K
King James 28
King's Men, The 28

L
London 5, 6, 28
Lord Chamberlain's Men, The 6
Love's Labour's Lost 10

M
Master of the Revels 14
Midsummer Night's Dream, A 6
Much Ado About Nothing 20

P
plague 16, 17, 18
plot 25
pomander 17
private performance 13
props 8, 15, 24

Q
Queen Elizabeth 13, 28

R
rats 10, 16
rehearsals 12, 13
revivals 14
Romeo and Juliet 12, 13

S
Shakespeare, William 6, 10, 12,
  14, 20, 22, 26
Shoreditch 5, 6

stage door 6
stocks 18

T
takings 8, 9, 13
text 14
thatch 27
Theatre, The 6, 20, 21, 22
tiremen 10
tiring house 24
traveling players 5, 18

W
women 8

A thousand times good night!